29

TURKEY RIDDLES

by Katy Hall and Lisa Eisenberg

pictures by Kristin Sorra

Dial Books for Young Readers • New York

Published by Dial Books for Young Readers
A division of Penguin Putnam Inc.
345 Hudson Street
New York, New York 10014

The Dial Easy-to-Read logo is a registered trademark of
Dial Books for Young Readers,
a division of Penguin Putnam Inc.
® TM 1,162,718.
3 5 7 9 10 8 6 4 2

Library of Congress Cataloging-in-Publication Data
Hall, Katy.
Turkey riddles/by Katy Hall and Lisa Eisenberg;
pictures by Kristin Sorra.
p. cm.
Summary: A collection of nearly three dozen riddles
featuring turkeys, such as "What happened when Tom Turkey
stepped up to the plate? He hit a fowl ball."
ISBN 0-8037-2530-2
1. Riddles, Juvenile. 2. Turkeys—Juvenile humor.
[1. Turkeys—Humor. 2. Riddles. 3. Jokes.]
I. Sorra, Kristin, ill. II. Title.
PN6371.5.H379   2002
398.6—dc21   2001047475

Reading Level 2.4

The art was drawn with pen and ink,
then scanned and colored in Photoshop.

What happened to the turkey
who ate too much corn?

He got an ear-ache.

What do you get if you cross a turkey with an octopus?

A Thanksgiving dinner with drumsticks for everyone!

What did the papa turkey say to the little turkey at supper time?

"Must you gobble, gobble, gobble your food?"

What did the vampire say to the turkey?

"Happy Fangs-giving!"

What costume did the little turkey wear every Halloween?

He was always a-gobblin'.

Why did the stuffing hide
behind the turkey?

It was dressing.

What happened when Tom
Turkey stepped up to the plate?

He hit a fowl ball.

What is Superturkey's real name?

Cluck Kent.

What do you call a gobbler in
a flowered shirt, plaid shorts,
and a beanie?

A *real* turkey!

What did the sweet potato say
to the turkey?

"Here I yam!"

How is a penny like a turkey sitting on a fence?

Head's on one side, and tail's on the other!

What happened when the fairy godmother waved her wand at the turkey?

She granted her wishbone.

What did the turkey say when
the Pilgrim passed the potatoes?

"No, thanks. I'm stuffed."

Why did Tom Turkey climb
into the vegetable bowl?

He wanted to rest in peas.

How do turkeys drink a toast
on New Year's Eve?

With gobble-lets.

Why did the turkey stuffing go on strike?

It wanted a higher celery!

What did the little turkey
say when he brought his dad
breakfast in bed?

"Happy Feather's Day!"

Why did the silly pig cover his ears when he passed the turkeys?

He didn't want to hear any fowl language.

How did the cook get locked
out of the kitchen?

All the tur-*keys* were inside.

What do you get if you cross a turkey with a bottle of glue?

Gobbledy-gook!

Do turkeys dance cheek to cheek?

No, beak to beak.

What's the difference between a turkey and an owl?

A turkey doesn't give a hoot.

What do turkeys sing when at birthday parties?

"Happy Bird-day to You!"

When is a turkey sorry to see her name in print?

When it's on a menu.

Why did the smart turkey carry an umbrella to work?

She'd watched the evening feather report!

What is a turkey's favorite day
to celebrate?

The day *after* Thanksgiving.

What did the turkey waiter say
to his customers?

"Wattle it be, folks?"

What do you call a turkey who cleans his house all day?

A feather duster!

Why did Mom Turkey tell
jokes to her eggs?

She wanted to crack them up!

Why isn't it safe for turkeys to do math?

If they add 3 and 5, they get ate!

What movie do little turkeys
like to watch?

The Gizzard of Oz.

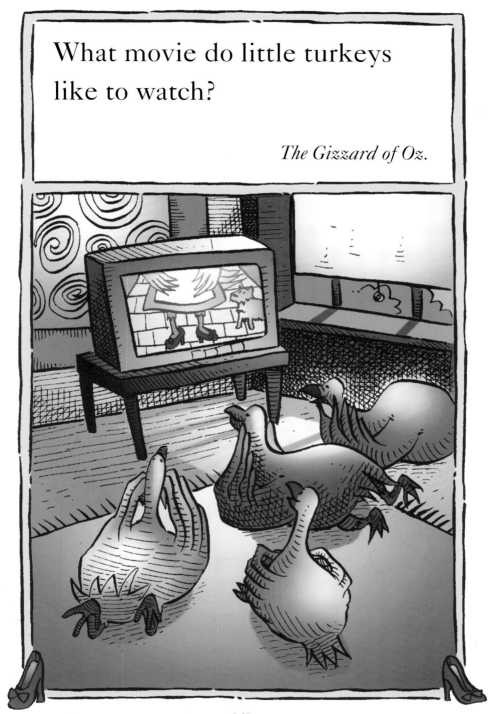

What do you call a super-hero turkey and his sidekick?

Beakman and Robin.

Why did the silly cat put her turkey in a ball gown?

She heard you were supposed to dress a turkey.

What's made of turkey and rice, comes in a can, and wears a cape?

Turkey Soup-erman!